Jokes from the Krusty Krab

Stephen Hillenburg

Based on the TV series *SpongeBob SquarePants*® created by Stephen Hillenburg as seen on Nickelodeon®

ISBN 0-439-76817-9

12 11 10 9 8 7 6 5 4 3 2 1   5 6 7 8 9 10/0

Printed in the U.S.A.   40

First Scholastic printing, September 2005

NICK

SpongeBob SquarePants

Jokes
from the
Krusty Krab

by David Lewman

SCHOLASTIC INC.

New York Toronto London Auckland Sydney
Mexico City New Delhi Hong Kong Buenos Aires

SpongeBob: What does food start out as?

Sandy: Baby food.

SpongeBob: What kind of food do you feed to sharks with your bare hands?

Squidward: Finger food.

When is food like Plankton?

When it goes bad.

SpongeBob: Why do fishermen like to fish where there are tons of mosquitoes?

Sandy: 'Cause they get lots of bites!

SpongeBob: Why should you never eat in a dirty house?

Squidward: Because you'll bite the dust.

What do you get when you eat a frozen Krabby Patty?

Frostbite.

5

Why did SpongeBob crawl under his food?

He doesn't like to overeat.

Why did Patrick refuse to crawl under the table?

He didn't want to be underfed.

What did SpongeBob say to the Krabby Patty?

"Pleased to eat you!"

What did the Krabby Patties say when they saw their friend in Patrick's hands?

"What's eating him?"

SpongeBob: What do you call a huge lizard that only eats in the evening?

Patrick: A dinnersaur.

Squidward: Did the spatula decide to catch the patty or drop it?

SpongeBob: It left it up in the air.

SpongeBob: Why did the customer step on his check?

Squidward: He wanted to foot the bill.

Squidward: Knock-knock.
Customer: Who's there?
Squidward: Men.
Customer: Men who?
Squidward: Menu, or are you ready to order?

Mr. Krabs: What's the difference between a wiener and someone who grabs all the spots?

SpongeBob: One's a hotdog and the other's a dot hog.

Mrs. Puff: Which fruit is the saddest?

SpongeBob: The blueberry.

Sandy: What did you lose at the Chum Bucket?

SpongeBob: My appetite.

CHUM BUCKET

SpongeBob: How did Patrick get food all over the mirror?

Squidward: He was trying to feed his face.

Patrick: What happened when the patty met the bun?

SpongeBob: It was lunch at first sight.

SpongeBob: What do you get when you cross a gull and a swallow?

Sandy: A sea gulp.

Patrick: Which part of the ocean is the thirstiest?

SpongeBob: The Gulp of Mexico.

SpongeBob: Knock-knock.
Customer: Who's there?
SpongeBob: Goblet.
Customer: Goblet who?
SpongeBob: Gobble it down—it's a Krabby Patty!

13

How did the Krabby Patty
feel when Squidward left
him on the grill too long?
It really burned him up.

Why did Patrick sign up for
percussion lessons?
Mr. Krabs told him to drum
up new business.

JELLYFISH JAM

Is it hard to guess Patrick's favorite dessert?

No, it's a piece of cake.

FRUITCaKE

Why did SpongeBob eat the Mystery Patty from the top down?

He wanted to get to the bottom of it.

Mr. Krabs: What did the restaurant owner say when the fisherman brought him free fish?

Squidward: "What's the catch?"

What's the difference between a mini-Krabby Patty and the sound a duck with a cold makes?

One's a quick snack and the other's a sick quack.

SpongeBob: Why did the frozen boy patty throw himself at the frozen girl patty?

Sandy: He wanted to break the ice.

Mr. Krabs: Why did you paint squares on the customer?

Patrick: Uh, because he said, "Check, please."

Why did SpongeBob throw paint during his fry cook's exam?

He wanted to pass with flying colors.

Patrick: Why can't boiling pots be spies?

SpongeBob: They always blow their covers.

Why did SpongeBob jump over the eating area?
Mr. Krabs told him to clear the table.

SpongeBob: Why did the soup refuse to leave the pot?
Sandy: It was chicken.

Mr. Krabs: Why do stand-up comics love to have eggs in their audiences?

SpongeBob: It's easy to make them crack up.

Why did Patrick bring a shovel to the Krusty Krab?

SpongeBob told him to dig in.

SpongeBob: How did the water feel after it washed the dishes?

Squidward: Drained.

What happened after Squidward said he'd never, ever eat alphabet soup?

He ate his words.

Patrick: How did the pancake's comedy act go over?
SpongeBob: It fell flat.

Patrick: How did that leave the pancake?
SpongeBob: Flat broke.

Why does Patrick fill his house with bread in the winter?

So it'll be nice and toasty.

Why did SpongeBob train a mouse to clean the Krusty Krab?

He wanted it to be squeaky clean.

Patrick: Why don't patties sleep on the grill?

SpongeBob: Because they'd spend the whole night tossing and burning.

Why did SpongeBob think the grill was angry?

It flared up at him.

Pearl: Why didn't the ketchup tell the mustard how he felt about her?

SpongeBob: His feelings were all bottled up.

Mr. Krabs: How did the ice cream react to leaving the freezer?

Squidward: It had a total meltdown.

SpongeBob: How did the napkin do in the poker game?

Squidward: It folded.

SpongeBob: What do you get when you cross a bird with a chili?

Squidward: A woodpepper.

Why did SpongeBob tie a rope to the seat and lift it to the ceiling?

Mr. Krabs told him to pull up a chair.

Pearl: Why was the pepper exhausted?

Mrs. Puff: Because it had been put through the mill.

Why did Mr. Krabs put all his money in the freezer?

Because he wanted cold cash.

Why was the patty grouchy?

It got up on the wrong side of the bread.

Patrick: How did the milkshake feel about his time in the blender?

SpongeBob: He had mixed feelings about it.

What's Plankton's favorite kind of bread?

Shortbread.

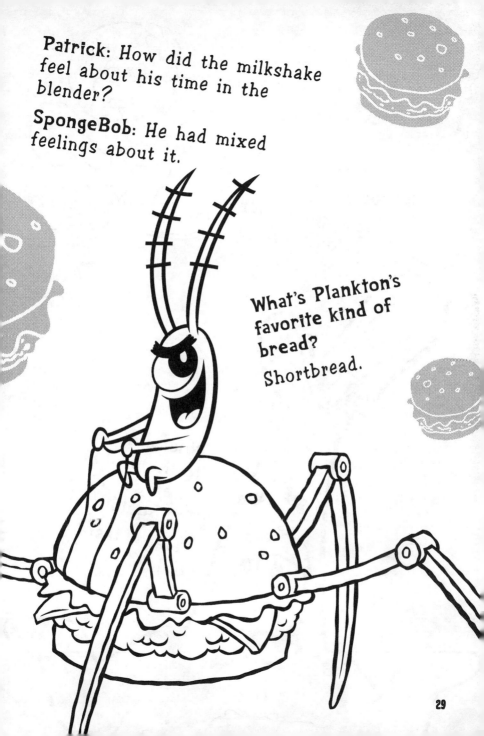

Sandy: When does butter do its best?

SpongeBob: When it's on a roll.

What did Patrick say to the customer when he filled in for Squidward?

"May I taste your order?"

Mr. Krabs: How did the onion feel about being sliced?

SpongeBob: It really got under his skin.

SpongeBob: When does food make you itch?

Patrick: When you make it from scratch.

How does SpongeBob say good-bye to the patties when he leaves work?

"Spatulater!"

Why did SpongeBob toss a sandwich at Sandy on her birthday?

He wanted to throw her a surprise patty.

Why did SpongeBob put a circle of Krusty Krab sandwiches around his house?

He wanted to have an outdoor patty-o.

What do they call a stall in the Krusty Krab restroom?

A Krabby Potty.

SpongeBob: Knock-knock.
Customer: Who's there?
SpongeBob: Stan.
Customer: Stan who?
SpongeBob: Stan in line to order, please.

SpongeBob: Knock-knock.
Squidward: Who's there?
SpongeBob: Betty.
Squidward: Betty who?
SpongeBob: Bet he orders another Krabby Patty.

Patrick: Knock-knock.
Squidward: Who's there?
Patrick: Al.
Squidward: Al who?
Patrick: Al have a double
    Krabby Patty with cheese.

Mr. Krabs: Knock-knock.
SpongeBob: Who's there?
Mr. Krabs: Donna.
SpongeBob: Donna who?
Mr. Krabs: Don a uniform
before you start work.

Patrick: Which big, mean fish bakes the best bread?

SpongeBob: The Great Wheat Shark.

Why did SpongeBob jump up on the stove? He wanted to play King of the Grill.

How would SpongeBob like working in a ship's kitchen?

It'd be right up his galley.

SpongeBob: What do you call a tortilla filled with ice?

Sandy: A brrr-ito.

SpongeBob: What do chickens eat when they wake up?
Sandy: Peckfast.

Why did Patrick attach four tires and a steering wheel to the table?

Because Mr. Krabs told him to bus it.

Mr. Krabs: What kind of cup is impossible to drink from?
Squidward: A hiccup.

Sandy: Why did the piece of corn try to join the army?
Squidward: Because he was already a kernel.

Patrick: What do ghosts order with their Krabby Patties?

SpongeBob: French frights.

Why did SpongeBob put a barbecue grill on the roof of his house?

He wanted to raise the steaks.

Sandy: Where do vegetables go to kiss?

SpongeBob: The mushroom.

Why did Patrick throw the T-bone in a blender?

He wanted to make a chocolate milksteak.

Why did Patrick try to have a conversation with a can of beans?

Because he'd heard there was a story called *Jack and the Beans Talk*.

SpongeBob: What do ducks eat for lunch?

Patrick: Quackaroni and cheese.

Sandy: What's green and comes on a bun?

Plankton: A hambooger.

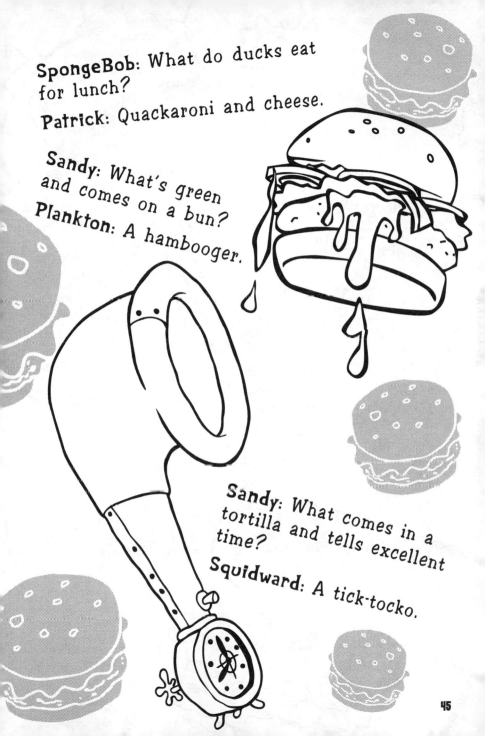

Sandy: What comes in a tortilla and tells excellent time?

Squidward: A tick-tocko.

SpongeBob: If corn could talk, what kind of voice would it have?

Mr. Krabs: Husky.

SpongeBob: What would it say?
Mr. Krabs: "Shucks, I'm all ears."

SpongeBob: What did the waiter say to the frog?

Squidward: "You want flies with that?"

What did SpongeBob say when he ran out of cabbage? "That's the last slaw."